I Love You Mom

AND HERE'S WHY

Mom,

There are things we think about the people we love, things we remember, things we don't always say. We store them in our hearts, but sometimes we keep them secret. I wanted to share those things with you in these pages because they make me happy, and I think it's time for you to know them, too. I'm grateful for everything we share.

With love always, Bean

....

These words make me think of you...

....

Smart
Funny
Sassy
Strong
Smart
Incredible
Bestest
smart
Beautiful
Entertaining
... did I say smart?
I am so lucky!

When people tell me I'm so much like you, it's usually because...

we're a

Cleverboots!

Whether tangible or intangible, there are so many things you've passed along to me. They remind me of where I've come from and where I'm going.

I think the best things I've inherited from you are...

a sharp, clever wit
a goofy, nonsensical sense of humor
a profound understanding and empathy
a love for all animals
well except bugs, obviously
a sensitivity and caring
a solid set of morals
a caring for all people and
a need to make things better

when I look at the best parts of me,
I see the best parts of you.

I'm pretty lucky, aren't I?

. . . .

Meals we've shared, music we listened to,
stories we loved, games we played—
there are so many things that make me think
of you, and the times we've spent together...

. . . .

all the times watching TV on the couch, from when I was young, back from the pool, and rewatching a video about construction trucks, to watching all the episodes of chopped after hours in one sitting, to the times we played skylanders, and the friendly cricket to rille matches on the floor, to the games around the breakfast table at the lake, dont Sammington to hamilton and singing like no one could hear us (we play it pretty loud- they might), to the time we played viva la viva ad nauseum, and running through the snow around lake harriet, to every dinner together, of pizza to nachos to the first time I tried salmon. my childhood has been an endless stream of memories that I will always cherish in my heart, and never forget,

I am the person I am today,
because of your love, your
support, your time, your heart,
your encouragement.

= I am the person I am because of you. =

This always makes me smile...
When I was younger, I thought you
could do anything because you...

It wasn't just the special occasions—you made every day something to remember.

These are some of the little things that meant a lot to me...

These places remind me of
some of my brightest, happiest
times. They're the places I
think of when I think of us...

You might be surprised to know that one of my favorite memories with you is...

There are people in
this world who make things
better wherever they go.

= Thank you for being one of them. =

I love the way we laugh, the jokes
we share, the silly things we do.

These are some of my favorites...

....

I've always admired how gifted you are at...

....

Even though I sometimes disagreed with you, when I look back now, I'm so grateful that you...

I think if you really wanted to,
you could...

I'm so glad I realized
it was possible for
you to be both my mother
and my friend.

Sometimes, the things you used to say
come to my mind at just the right moments.
It's like you're right here, reminding me...

You taught me this by your
own example, and it's something
I've never forgotten...

You just might be the only
person who can...

. . . .

You have your own ways of being strong.
One of my favorite things about you is the
way you aren't afraid to...

. . . .

There is beauty in your
words and your actions, your
spirit and your strength,
your courageousness and
your heart.

= It's in all that you are and everything you do. =

Looking back, I don't know
how you found the energy, but
you always managed to...

Every day, just by the way
you live and love, you show
me what matters most.

You taught me that the most important things are...

There are still so many things for us to see and try and do. Some of the dreams I have for us are...

If I could give you anything
in the world, it would be...

You deserve it.

You give me a love with a
future built in, a love
that can span any distance,
a love with a capacity for
everything we will become.

I've never told you this, but
I want you to know...

COMPENDIUM®
live inspired.

With special thanks to the entire Compendium family.

CREDITS:

Written by: M.H. Clark
Designed by: Heidi Rodriguez
Edited by: Amelia Riedler
Creative Direction by: Julie Flahiff

ISBN: 978-1-938298-55-4

2nd printing. Printed in China with soy inks.